BEN FOLDS ADDS MUSIC AND MELODY TO NICK HORNBY'S WORDS

LONELY AVENUE

T0052904

Produced by
Alfred Music Publishing Co., Inc.
P.O. Box 10003
Van Nuys, CA 91410-0003
alfred.com

Printed in USA.

No part of this book shall be reproduced, arranged, adapted, recorded, publicly performed, stored in a retrieval system, or transmitted by any means without written permission from the publisher. In order to comply with copyright laws, please apply for such written permission and/or license by contacting the publisher at alfred.com/permissions.

ISBN-10: 0-7390-7704-X
ISBN-13: 978-0-7390-7704-7

Cover Photograph by Joel Meyerowitz; Photographs of Ben Folds & Nick Hornby by Michael Wilson; Design by John Heiden for Smog Design, Inc.

 Alfred Cares. Contents printed on 100% recycled paper.

LONELY AVENUE

CONTENTS

LYRICS

A WORKING DAY

I can do this
Really
I'm good enough
I'm as good as them
Don't take it from me
Ask my friends
Ask my sister
They all think my stuff is great
Up there with any of them
I just need a break

I'm a genius
Really
I'm excellent
Better than them
I kicked their asses
All of them
Even that guy who thinks he's so fucking cool
And gets all the attention
He doesn't sell shit does he?

Some guy on the net thinks I suck
And he should know
He's got his own blog

I'm a loser, I'm a poser
Yeah really, it's over
I mean it and I quit
Everything I write is shit

I'm a loser and a poser
Yeah really, it's over
Hey hey
It's a working day
Hey hey
It's a working day

PICTURE WINDOW

They checked into the hospital New Year's
Eve
Nothing to be done about that
Rainbows, daffodils, she's not naive
Symbolism's all crap

There's a big picture window in their room
on the ward
With a view over Parliament Hill
But the view offers more joy than they can
afford
When there's this much pain to kill

You know what hope is? Hope is a bastard
Hope is a liar, a cheat and a tease
Hope comes near you, kick its backside
Got no place in days like these

At dusk the darkness surrenders to colour
As the fireworks streak the sky
And their window gives them the prettiest
picture
The useless luck makes her want to cry

You know what hope is? Hope is a bastard
Hope is a liar, a cheat and a tease
Hope comes near you, kick its backside
Got no place in days like these

Then it turns midnight, the shitty old year's
spent
Another mum gives her some sparkling wine
She nearly gives in to the moment
But he'll still be sick in 2009

You know what hope is? Hope is a bastard
Hope is a liar, a cheat and a tease
Hope comes near you, kick its backside
Got no place in days like these

And just as she's thinking of pulling the blind
down
A huge rocket bursts, right in front of her eyes
The city lit up, London's given a bright crown
As she tries, and fails, to stop spirits rise

You know what hope is? Hope is a bastard
Hope is a liar, a cheat and a tease
Hope comes near you, kick its backside
Got no place in days like these

LEVI JOHNSTON'S BLUES

Woke up this morning, what do I see?
Three thousand cameras, pointing at me
Dude says, You Levi? I'm like, Yes, that's me,
sir!
"Well, you've knocked up the VP nominee's
daughter"

So I tell him, No, you got it wrong, mister
Already with a girl, and her name's Bristol
They all laugh and say, Where you been,
sonny?
Your mother-in-law's a heartbeat from the
presidency

I say, Mother-in-law? No, we ain't getting
married
They say, You will be soon, boy, she just
announced it
I get on my dirt bike, ride to my girl's home
I'm gonna lay down the law, tell her what's
going on

I'm a fuckin' redneck, I live to hang out with
the boys
Play some hockey, do some fishing, kill some
moose
I like to shoot the shit and do some chillin',
I guess
Ya fuck with me and I'll kick your ass

So we talk and it turns out we don't believe
in abortion
And sex outside marriage is against our
religion
And when I try to tell them I'm eighteen
years old
They say, Levi, it's too late, you gotta do as
you're told

I'm a fuckin' redneck, I live to hang out with
the boys
Get on my snowboard, do some fishing, kill
some moose
I like to shoot the shit and do some chillin',
I guess
Ya fuck with me and I'll kick your ass

DOC POMUS

Man in a wheelchair in the lobby of the
Forrest
With frighters, hustlers, hard-up millionaires
Mobsters, cops, whores, pimps and Marxists
All human life is there

Man in a wheelchair listens to the chatter
Writes down all the insane crap he hears
He can't move around but it doesn't really
matter
In the Forrest all you need is eyes and ears

And out they pour, the hits and misses
Turn Me Loose, Lonely Avenue
And down in Nashville Elvis sings Suspicion
Pomus/Shuman, 1962

And he never could be one of those happy
cripples
The kind that smile and tell you life's OK
He was mad as hell, frightened and bitter
He found a way to make his feelings pay

Back at the Forrest, in the steakhouse off
the lobby
Another diner gets three bullets in the head
Doc looks down and carries on eating his
linguine
Tries to think up a lyric for the dead

Fred Neil, Jack Benny, and crazy Phil Spector
Pumpkin Juice and Eydie Gormé
Damon Runyon Jr. and the Duke's orchestra
All superhuman life was there

And he never could be one of those happy
cripples
The kind that smile and tell you life's OK
He was mad as hell, frightened and bitter
He found a way to make his isolation pay

YOUR DOGS

I see it all, I get it, I promise you I do
Your mom walked out on you when you were
only two
You've grown up believing that this country
hates the poor
You're a dad three times over and you're only
twenty-four

The Christians on the radio, they act like
you're scum
Self-righteous condescending bastards, each
and every one
I don't read the Bible but I try to love you,
man
Every flaw and violent act, I think I under-
stand

But your dogs, your dogs, what's fun about
those?
And that tat on your neck, and that ring
through your nose?
The weed, the junk food, the violent
pornography
You don't think you'd want to be
Just a little bit more like me?

I still have high hopes you could join our
community
There's more of us than you now, but we'd
welcome
 the diversity
You're not white trash, like the other neigh-
bours say
If you want to challenge stereotyping, join
the PTA

At night, when your pit bulls are scaring our
children
My wife, I'll be honest here, wants me to
.shoot them
And sometimes I let my fantasies run

But that's only at night, when I'm not really
thinking
And you're listening to Metallica in your
backyard
 and drinking
The rest of the time I think we get along fine
I never judge you, I'm a live-and-let-live guy

But your dogs, your dogs, what's fun about
those?
And that tat on your neck, and that ring
through your nose?
The weed, the junk food, the violent
pornography
You don't think you'd want to be
Just a little bit more like me?

PRACTICAL AMANDA

Who'd look at that dump and see a home?
Why not move in somewhere easy?
Urinals where bedrooms should be
Who could be bothered, really?

You're really good at all that stuff
The nuts and bolts of living
Curtains, blinds and kitchen tables

I've got no time for dates and plans
I'm too busy dreaming
You've got the attention span
You're not the freewheeler

Practical Amanda
Practical Amanda
Saved one life and made two others
Practical Amanda

Who'd look in here and see someone
That might be worth redeeming?
Head and heart and soul fucked up
Who could be bothered, really?

I've got no time for dates and plans
I'm too busy dreaming
You've got the attention span
Practical Amanda

Practical Amanda
Practical Amanda
Saved one life and made two others
Practical Amanda

CLAIRE'S NINTH

So
She stands
And waits
And waits at the school gate

They're late
They come
—so dumb!—
In two cars
When they agreed one

So they fight
And it's gone wrong
On her birthday

So
They go
To Joe's
For pizza and ice cream

They sit
And stare
And Claire
Just wants to
Be nine and a half

Next year she'll tell them
She doesn't want anything
Except world peace

But Claire
Claire baby
I wish you knew
How this all got twisted
I wish you could see
Right inside us
There's all this stuff
The best of us
That we can't get out

What's
The point
Of this?
What's wrong with two birthdays?

It's cool
At school
Her friends
They all have two birthdays

Oh Jeez
He just asked the waitress
Out on a date
On her birthday

But Claire
Claire baby
I wish you knew
How this all got twisted
I wish you could see
Right inside us
There's all this stuff
The best of us
That we can't get to

Here's
The check
They pay
With two cards like they've never met

Goodbyes
Outside
It's cold in LA

But Claire
Claire baby
I wish you knew
How this got all twisted
I wish you could see
Right inside us

You're the best of us
The most of us
You're what we were
You're all that's left
It used to be
Our birthday too

LYRICS

PASSWORD

I know you
You think I don't, but I do
I've been listening, and I don't forget
So I can do this, I can pass this test

You went to school in CHICAGO
Your mum's maiden name was DUPREE
Your favourite actor is DE NIRO
Your birthday's 03.08.83

I know you
You'll think it's weird, but it's not
You are looking at it all upside-down
It actually means I really love you

You used to have a dog called MONTY
You only drink CHARDONNAY
Your sister's pet name is CEE CEE
You have a thing for David BLAINE

I know you
You think I'm blind, but I'm not
I've been watching, and what I notice
Is distraction, boredom, vacancy

Your favourite dish is PRIMAVERA
You like the Polyphonic SPREE
You spent a year in BARCELONA
That asshole's name is ANTHONY (Ding!)

Turns out you never went to TULSA
To see your old roommate JANE
I think my middle name is SUCKER
I was born YESTERDAY

I don't know you
I thought I did, but I don't
I wasn't listening, not to the right things
One day I won't even remember your face

FROM ABOVE

They even looked at each other once
Across a crowded bar
He was with Martha
She was with Tom
Neither of them knew what was going on
A strange feeling of never
Heartbeats becoming synchronized
And staying that way forever

But most of the time
It was just near misses
Air kisses
Once in a bookstore, once at a party
She came in just as he was leaving
And years ago, at the movies, she sat behind him
A six-thirty showing of *While You Were Sleeping*
He never once looked round

It's so easy from above
You can really see it all
People who belong together
Lost and sad and small
But there's nothing to be done for them
It doesn't work that way
Sure, we all have soul mates
But we walk past them every day

And it's not like they were ever actually unhappy
In the lives they lived
He married Martha
She married Tom
Just this vague notion that something was wrong
An ache, an absence, a phantom limb
An itch that could never be scratched

And who knows whether that's how it should be
Maybe our ghosts live right in that vacancy

It's so easy from above
You can really see it all
People who belong together
Lost and sad and small
But there's nothing to be done for them
It doesn't work that way
Sure, we all have soul mates
But we walk past them every day

Maybe that's how books get written
Maybe that's why songs get sung
Maybe we owe the unlucky ones

SASKIA HAMILTON

I've only ever seen her name on a spine
But that's enough, I want to make her mine
Never heard her voice, never seen her smile
But I'm in love with Saskia Hamilton...

Well she's a poet, just like I want to be
But her passport alone is great poetry

She got more assonance than she knows what to do with
I'm in love with Saskia Hamilton
She got two sibilants, no bilabial plosives
I'm in love with Saskia Hamilton

Saskia Hamilton, Saskia Hamilton
Saskia, Saskia, Saskia Hamilton

Already have a girl but she sounds real bad
I'm in love with Saskia Hamilton
She got alliteration and her surname is Dagg

No hard consonants in my girl Saskia
Every single syllable sounds like Shakespeare
I'm in love with Saskia Hamilton

Gonna live with her and it'll all be harmonious
How could it not be, when she's that euphonious?
Gonna marry her and it'll all be idyllic
AND MY TEACHER JUST TOLD ME THAT SHE'S DACTYLIC!

Saskia Hamilton, Saskia Hamilton
Saskia, Saskia, Saskia Hamilton

BELINDA

Every night around this time he has to sing
"Belinda"
"Belinda I love you / Don't leave me / I need you"
He tried to stop, a while back, but what is he, without her?
A one-hit wonder with no hits is what he is

And anyway he always hears how much it means to people
There's a lot of fortysomethings wouldn't be in the world
 without it
So now he has to do it with this lyric in his head

Belinda I loved you
And I'm sorry
I left you
I met somebody younger on a plane
She had big breasts
And a nice smile
No kids, either
She gave me extra complimentary champagne

No one ever wants to hear the song he wrote for Cindy
"Cindy I love you / I need you / Don't leave me"
And he can't blame them—they can tell his heart was
 never in it
And Cindy never liked it, but she never much liked him

Belinda I loved you
And I'm sorry
I left you
I met somebody younger on a plane
She had big breasts
And a nice smile
No kids, either
She gave me extra complimentary champagne

So every night about this time he feels the old self-loathing
While the old folks in the audience sing along
And he smiles and waves the mike at them so they can do
 the chorus
He's not there
He's somewhere else
He's with Belinda in the days before he made it all go wrong

Belinda I love you
She gave me complimentary champagne

A WORKING DAY

Words by
NICK HORNBY

Music by
BEN FOLDS

Verse:

1. I can do this. Real-ly, I'm good e-nough. I'm as good as them,_ but don't take it from me.
2. I'm a gen - ious. Real-ly, I'm ex-cel - lent. Bet-ter than them. I___ kicked_their a** - es.___

Ask my friends, ask my sis - ter. They all think my stuff is great,
All of them, e - ven that guy_____ who thinks he's f*** - ing cool,

up there, with an - y of them.___ I just need a break.
gets all of the at - ten - tion. He does - n't sell sh**, does he?

A Working Day - 4 - 1

© 2010 WARNER-TAMERLANE PUBLISHING CORP., FREE FROM THE MAN SONGS, LLC and UNIVERSAL MUSIC-CAREERS
All Rights on behalf of itself and FREE FROM THE MAN SONGS, LLC Administered by WARNER-TAMERLANE PUBLISHING CORP.
All Rights Reserved

Chorus:

Some guy on the net___ thinks I suck, and he should know.___ He's got his own blog.___

Some guy on the net___ thinks I suck, and he should know.___ He's

PICTURE WINDOW

Words by
NICK HORNBY

Music by
BEN FOLDS

© 2010 WARNER-TAMERLANE PUBLISHING CORP., FREE FROM THE MAN SONGS, LLC and UNIVERSAL MUSIC-CAREERS
All Rights on behalf of itself and FREE FROM THE MAN SONGS, LLC Administered by WARNER-TAMERLANE PUBLISHING CORP.
All Rights Reserved

as the fi-re-works streak the sky._____ And their

win-dow gives them the pret-ti-est pic-ture. The use-less luck makes her

want to cry._____ Then it turns mid-night, the sh**-ty old year's_ spent. An-oth-er

mum gives her_ some spar-kling wine. And she near-ly gives

Chorus:

LEVI JOHNSTON'S BLUES

Words by
NICK HORNBY

Music by
BEN FOLDS

Levi Johnston's Blues - 9 - 1

© 2010 WARNER-TAMERLANE PUBLISHING CORP., FREE FROM THE MAN SONGS, LLC and UNIVERSAL MUSIC-CAREERS
All Rights on behalf of itself and FREE FROM THE MAN SONGS, LLC Administered by WARNER-TAMERLANE PUBLISHING CORP.
All Rights Reserved

22

like to shoot the sh** and do some chill-in', I guess.___ Ya f*** with me,___ and I'll kick your ass.___

To Coda ⊕

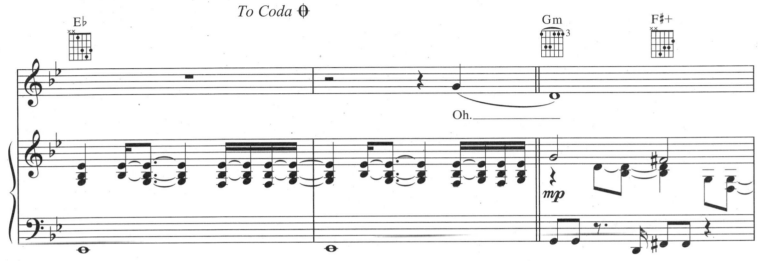

Oh.___

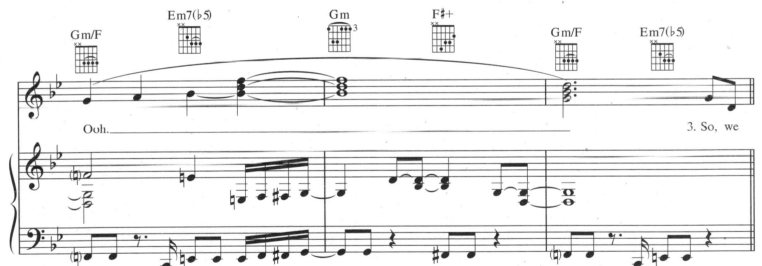

Ooh.___   3. So, we

Verse 3:

talk and it turns out we don't be - lieve in a - bor - tion,   and sex out - side mar - riage   is a -

Levi Johnston's Blues - 9 - 4

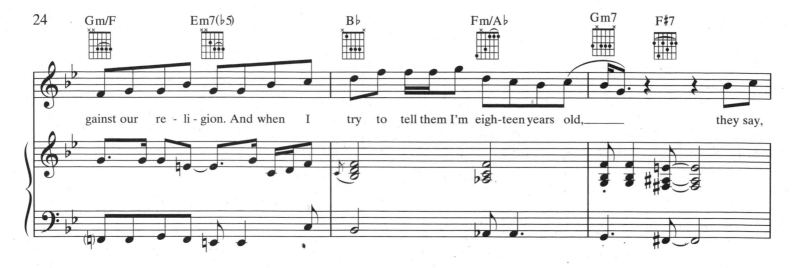

gainst our re - li - gion. And when I try to tell them I'm eigh-teen years old,_____ they say,

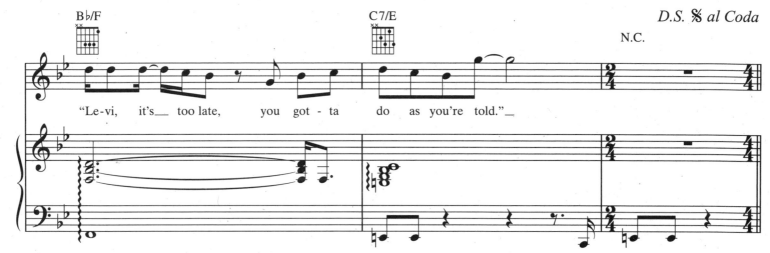

"Le-vi, it's__ too late, you got - ta do as you're told."__

D.S. 𝄋 al Coda

N.C.

Φ Coda

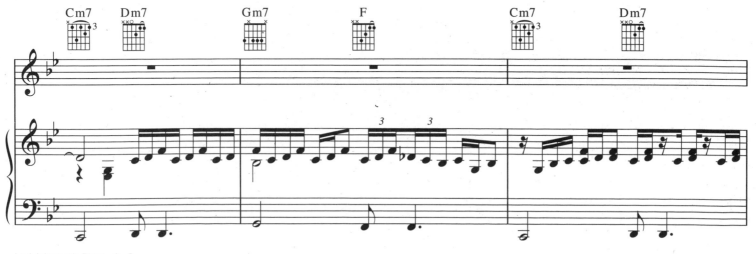

I'm a f***-in' red-neck. I live to hang out with the boys,_

_ get on my snow-board, do some fish-ing, and kill some moose._

I like to shoot the sh** and do some chill-in', I guess._ Ya

f*** with me,_ and I'll kick your ass._

like to shoot the sh** and do some chill-in', I guess.___ Ya f*** with me,___ and I'll kick your ass.___

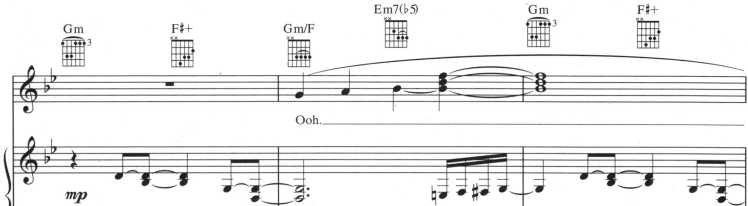

Ooh._____

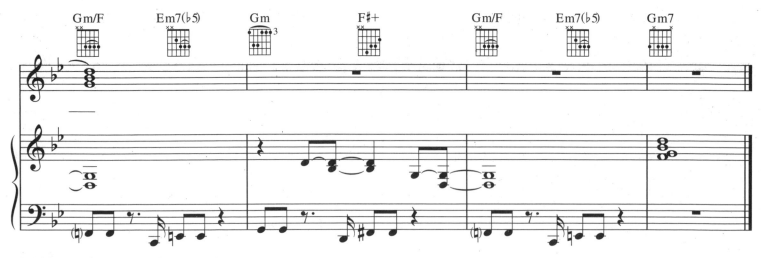

DOC POMUS

Words by
NICK HORNBY

Music by
BEN FOLDS

Moderately bright ♩ = 144

Verse 1:

1. Man in a wheel-chair, lob-by of the For-rest, with

fright-ers, hus-tlers, hard-up mil-lion-aires.

Doc Pomus - 15 - 1

© 2010 WARNER-TAMERLANE PUBLISHING CORP., FREE FROM THE MAN SONGS, LLC and UNIVERSAL MUSIC-CAREERS
All Rights on behalf of itself and FREE FROM THE MAN SONGS, LLC Administered by WARNER-TAMERLANE PUBLISHING CORP.
All Rights Reserved

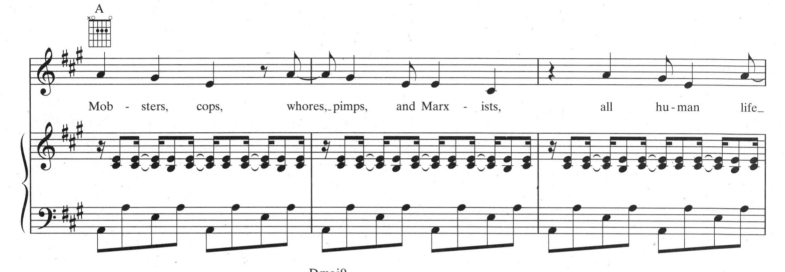

Mob - sters, cops, whores,_ pimps, and Marx - ists, all hu - man life_

_ is there._____

Man in a wheel-chair lis -

tens to the chat-ter, writes down all___ the in - sane crap___ he

Dmaj9

hears.

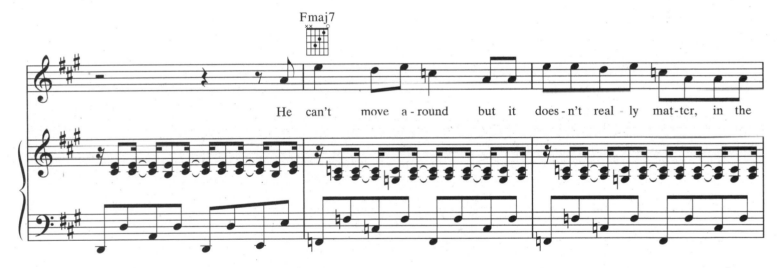

Fmaj7

He can't move a-round but it does-n't real-ly mat-ter, in the

Dmaj9

For-rest, all___ you need___ is eyes___ and ears.

And out_

Chorus:

A   A/G♯   F♯m7   F♯m7/E   Dmaj9

_ they pour, the hits___ and the miss-es. Turn me loose, Lone-

(French Horn)

E6   A   A/G♯   F♯m7   F♯m7/E

ly Av-e-nue. And down__ in Nash-ville, El-vis sings "Sus-pi-cion."

tell you life's o - kay. (Ah._____

_____) He was mad as hell,___ fright-

ened and bit - ter, he found a way___ to make___ his feel - ings

Dmaj9

pay. (Ah._____)

Fmaj7

Back at the For-rest in the steak-house off the lob - by, a

Dmaj9

din - er gets__ three bul - lets in__ the head.__

(Bop bop_ bop   bop.__)

Doc looks down, eat-ing his lin-gui-ne, think-ing up__ a lyr-ic for__ the dead.__

Chorus:

And out__ they pour, the hits__

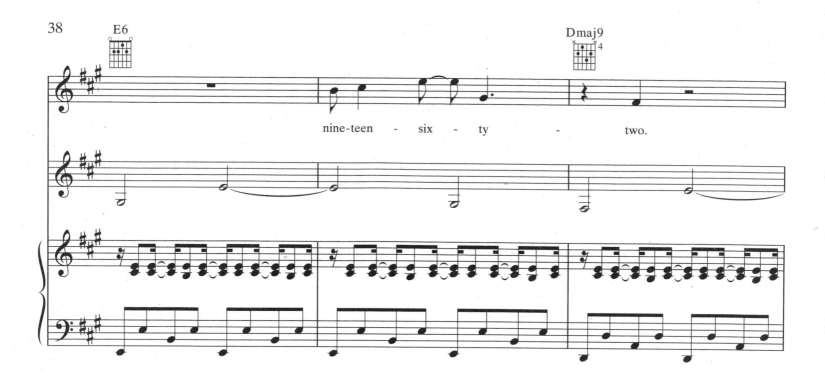

nine-teen - six - ty - two.

Bridge:

Fred Neil, Jack Ben - ny, cra - zy

nine-teen - six - ty - two.

(Organ)

YOUR DOGS

Words by
NICK HORNBY

Music by
BEN FOLDS

© 2010 WARNER-TAMERLANE PUBLISHING CORP., FREE FROM THE MAN SONGS, LLC and UNIVERSAL MUSIC-CAREERS
All Rights on behalf of itself and FREE FROM THE MAN SONGS, LLC Administered by WARNER-TAMERLANE PUBLISHING CORP.
All Rights Reserved

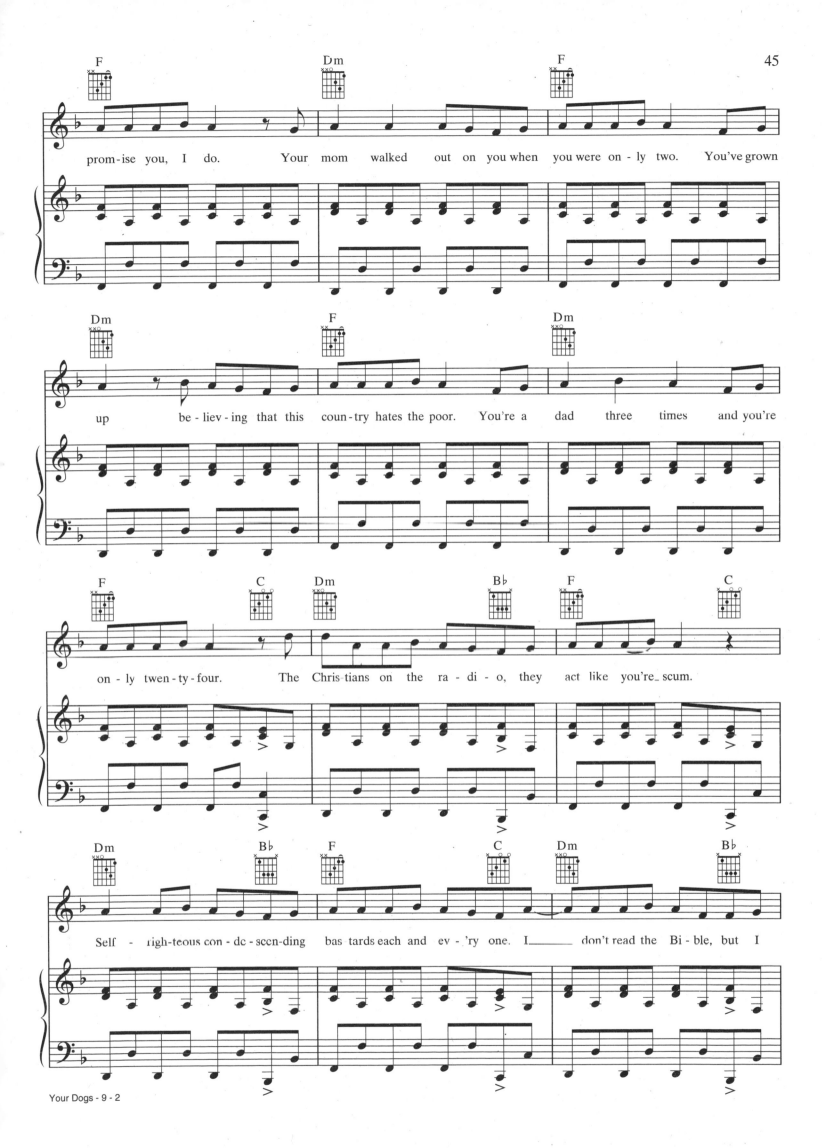

prom-ise you, I do. Your mom walked out on you when you were on-ly two. You've grown

up be-liev-ing that this coun-try hates the poor. You're a dad three times and you're

on-ly twen-ty-four. The Chris-tians on the ra-di-o, they act like you're scum.

Self - right-eous con-de-scend-ing bas-tards each and ev-'ry one. I____ don't read the Bi-ble, but I

try to love you, man. Ev-'ry flaw and vio-lent act I think I un-der-stand. But your

Chorus:

dogs, your dogs, what's fun a-bout those? The tat on your neck and the

ring through your nose? The weed, the junk food, the vio-lent por-nog-ra-phy?

Don't you think you want to be_____ just a lit-tle more like

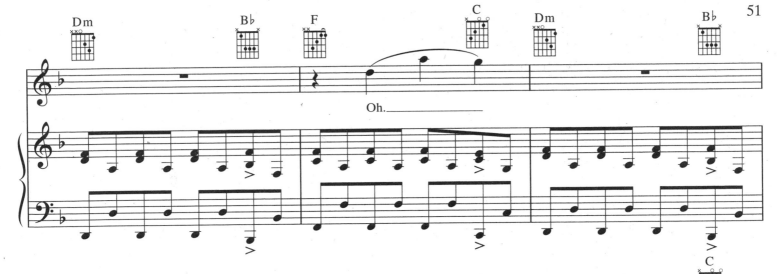

52

PRACTICAL AMANDA

Words by
NICK HORNBY

Music by
BEN FOLDS

Practical Amanda - 5 - 1

© 2010 WARNER-TAMERLANE PUBLISHING CORP., FREE FROM THE MAN SONGS, LLC and UNIVERSAL MUSIC-CAREERS
All Rights on behalf of itself and FREE FROM THE MAN SONGS, LLC Administered by WARNER-TAMERLANE PUBLISHING CORP.
All Rights Reserved

Prac - ti - cal___ A - man - da.___

CLAIRE'S NINTH

Words by
NICK HORNBY

Music by
BEN FOLDS

Claire's Ninth - 9 - 1

© 2010 WARNER-TAMERLANE PUBLISHING CORP., FREE FROM THE MAN SONGS, LLC and UNIVERSAL MUSIC-CAREERS
All Rights on behalf of itself and FREE FROM THE MAN SONGS, LLC Administered by WARNER-TAMERLANE PUBLISHING CORP.
All Rights Reserved

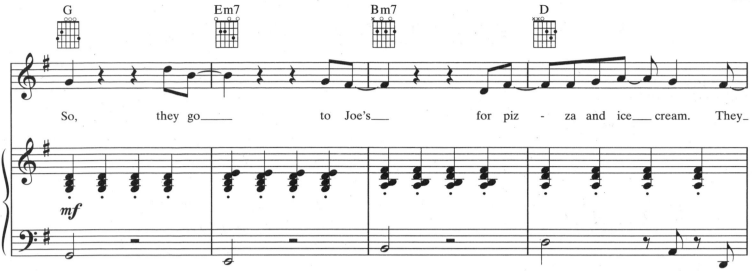

So, they go_____ to Joe's_____ for piz - za and ice__ cream. They__

__ sit and stare,___ and Claire___ just wants__ to be nine__ and a half.__

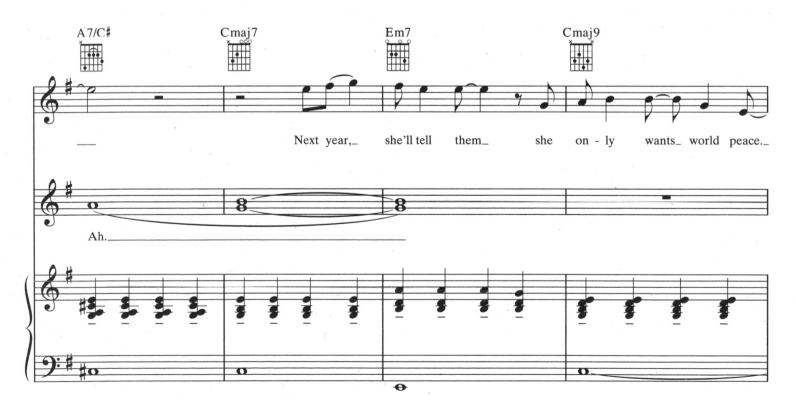

__ Next year,__ she'll tell them__ she on - ly wants__ world peace.__

Ah._____

Chorus:

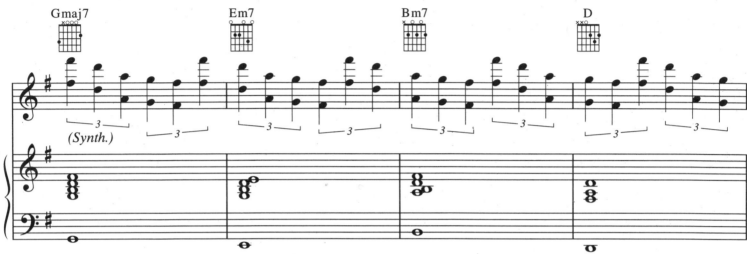

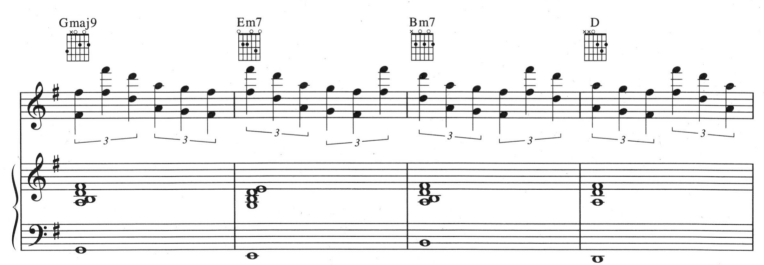

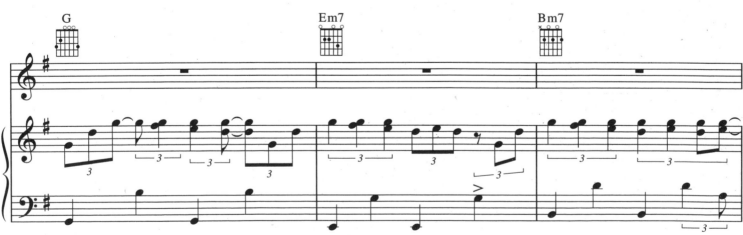

𝄌 *Coda*

of us.__ You're what__ we__ were,_ you're all__ that's left.__ It used_

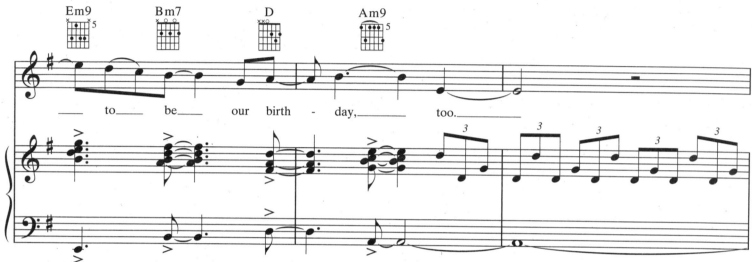

to__ be__ our birth - day,_____ too._____

Fade out

FROM ABOVE

Words by
NICK HORNBY

Music by
BEN FOLDS

Verse 1:

looked at each oth - er once___ a - cross a crowd - ed bar.

From Above - 11 - 1

© 2010 WARNER-TAMERLANE PUBLISHING CORP., FREE FROM THE MAN SONGS, LLC and UNIVERSAL MUSIC-CAREERS
All Rights on behalf of itself and FREE FROM THE MAN SONGS, LLC Administered by WARNER-TAMERLANE PUBLISHING CORP.
All Rights Reserved

kiss-es, once in a book-store, once at a par-ty; she came in as he was leav-in'.___ And years a-go, at the mov-ies, she sat be-hind___ him,___ a six-thir-ty show-in' of "While You Were Sleep-ing;" he nev-er once looked a-round.___ It's so

𝄋 *Chorus:*

easy from above,___ you can real-ly see it all;___ peo-ple who be-long___ to-geth-er,___ lost and sad and small.___ But there's noth-in' to be done___ for them;___ it does-n't work___ that way.___ Sure, we all___ have soul mates, but we walk past___ them ev-'ry day,___ oh,___ no.___

To Coda ✛

Verse 2:

like they were ev - er ac - tu-'lly un - hap - py in the lives___ they lived.__

He mar-ried Mar - tha; she mar-ried Tom.__ Just___ this vague_

2. And it's not

Bridge:

Nei - ther of___ them knew___ what was go - in' on;___ a strange feel - in' of

nev - er, heart-beats be - com - in' syn - chro - nized_ and stay - in' that way for - ev -

er.

who be-long_ to-geth - er,___ lost and sad and small.__ But there's

noth-in' to be done__ for them;_ it does-n't work_ that way.__ Sure, we all_

__ have soul_ mates, but we walk past__ them ev - 'ry day,___ oh,__ no._

May-be that's_ how books_ get writ-ten. May-be that's_ why songs_ get sung.

PASSWORD

Words by
NICK HORNBY

Music by
BEN FOLDS

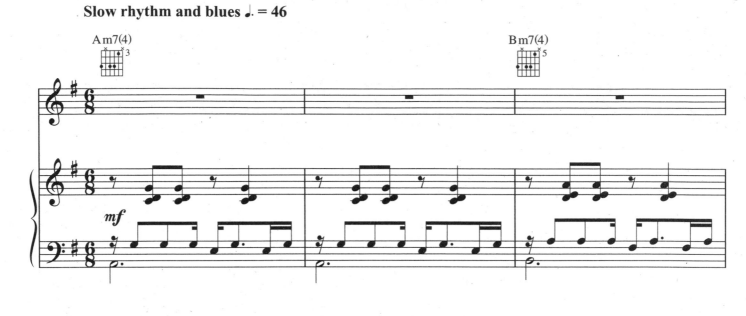

© 2010 WARNER-TAMERLANE PUBLISHING CORP., FREE FROM THE MAN SONGS, LLC and UNIVERSAL MUSIC-CAREERS
All Rights on behalf of itself and FREE FROM THE MAN SONGS, LLC Administered by WARNER-TAMERLANE PUBLISHING CORP.
All Rights Reserved

on - ly drink Char-don-nay. Your sis-ter's pet name__ is Cee Cee.__

You have a thing for Da-vid Blaine. 2. Ooh,__

Chorus 2:

hoo,__ M - o - n -

t - y. Ooh,__ hoo,__ C - h -

Chorus 3:

BELINDA

Words by
NICK HORNBY

Music by
BEN FOLDS

© 2010 WARNER-TAMERLANE PUBLISHING CORP., FREE FROM THE MAN SONGS, LLC and UNIVERSAL MUSIC-CAREERS
All Rights on behalf of itself and FREE FROM THE MAN SONGS, LLC Administered by WARNER-TAMERLANE PUBLISHING CORP.
All Rights Reserved

Verse 2:

2. No one ev - er wants to hear the song he wrote for Cin - dy. "Cin -

a tempo

dy, I love you. I need you. Don't leave me." And

he can't blame them; they can tell his heart was nev - er in it. And Cin -

dy nev - er liked it. But she nev - er much liked him. Be - lin -

Verse 3:

3. So ev - 'ry night__ a - bout__ this time,__ he

feels the old__ self - loath - ing__ while the old folks in the au - di - ence sing a - long.

And he smiles and waves__ the mic__ at them,__ so

She gave____ me com - pli - men - ta - ry___ cham -

pagne. She gave____ me com - pli - men - ta - ry___ cham -

pagne. Oh!

SASKIA HAMILTON

Words by
NICK HORNBY

Music by
BEN FOLDS

1. I've on-ly ev-er seen her name on a spine,_ but that's e-nough._ I want to make her mine.

Nev-er heard her voice, nev-er seen her smile, but I'm in love with Sas-ki-a Ham-il-ton.

Saskia Hamilton - 7 - 1

© 2010 WARNER-TAMERLANE PUBLISHING CORP., FREE FROM THE MAN SONGS, LLC and UNIVERSAL MUSIC-CAREERS
All Rights on behalf of itself and FREE FROM THE MAN SONGS, LLC Administered by WARNER-TAMERLANE PUBLISHING CORP.
All Rights Reserved

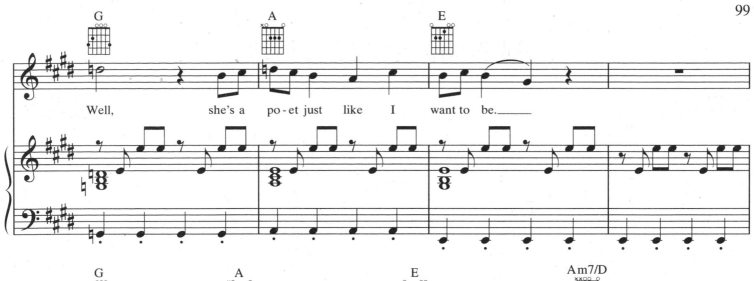

Well, she's a po-et just like I want to be._____

But her pass-port a-lone is great po-et-ry._____ And I'm in love with

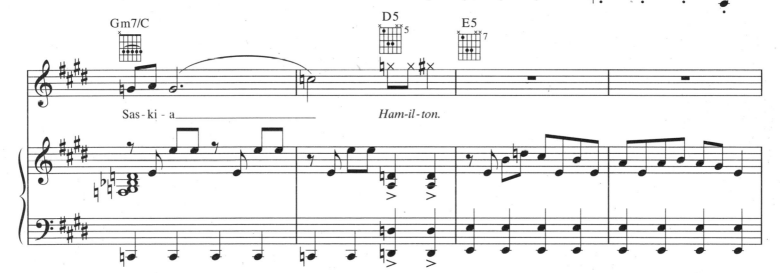

Sas-ki-a_____ *Ham-il-ton.*

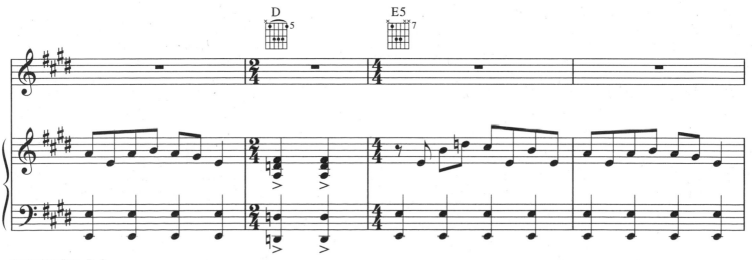

Verse 3:

Bridge:

(Inst. and vocal ad lib....

...end ad lib.)